What others are saying a

His Pe

MW00638446

"Peace is not the absence or conflict; it is the presence of God in the life of a Christian. In these devotionals, Neil Carmichael takes us on a journey to the place of Jesus' transforming peace. Meditate on the scripture, savor Neil's thoughts, linger with the daily prayer. You will be blessed!"

— ROBERT WHITLOW
Best-selling author of *The Choice*

"Deep, biblical, and practical. I should also add 'personal,' given that Neil Carmichael shares these powerful truths from his heart. *His Peace for Your Life* is the perfect 31-day push into a sweeter, more profound fellowship with your Savior – I highly recommend it!"

— JONI EARECKSON TADA
Joni and Friends International Disability Center

"Godliness with contentment is great gain." One of the blessings of the Christian life is peace. As Carmichael shows, this is not a passive peace, but a proactive campaign to rest in God's World with God's Ways. You will enjoy this daily reminder of what we have in Christ in the midst of a busy and, at times, threatening world."

— ANDY PETERSON, Ph.D.
President, Reformed Theological Seminary, Global

"An important spiritual practice is known as the "examen." It's the practice of reviewing our lives, day by day, and asking: where have I sensed God? Where have I missed him? Where have I had joy? or discouragement. These pithy and thoughtful (and heartfelt) devotionals by Neil Carmichael are real to life, and real to faith. They will help you look at your life in terms of God's plan and peace - sometimes mysterious, always in the end fruitful."

— LEIGHTON FORD
Leighton Ford Ministries

"Jesus, the One who makes all things possible, makes it possible for us to be at peace no matter our circumstances. Neil Carmichael's devotional, *His Peace for Your Life*, eloquently captures this truth. It is an everyday devotional for everyday life. I loved it all!"

— MARK SCHULTZ
Contemporary Christian Recording Artist

"Neil's daily insights, drawn from his personal illustrations and biblical discernment, challenge us to evaluate our peace and contentment from God's viewpoint. He takes us on a month-long journey where we come to see God in a new way. As Neil's Pastor and friend, I know he lives it and wants the reader to live it too - it's seen in the warmth and devotion to each scripture and story. This contemplative work will strengthen your time in prayer and bring your faith to action."

— CHRIS PAYNE
Lead Pastor, New Charlotte Church

"*His Peace for Your Life* is a profound and eloquent masterpiece by a gifted teacher and writer. I believe that Carmichael's work has the potential to become a classic. Each daily devotional offers enough quality content to satisfy spiritual appetites without overload."

— GENE GETZ
Ph.D., Professor, Pastor and Author

"There are three dimensions to the peace that God offers to us through Christ: peace with God, peace with one another, and peace within ourselves. This superb devotional touches repeatedly on each dimension, guiding our feet onto paths of peace!"

— KEN SANDE
Founder of Peacemaker Ministries and Relational Wisdom 360

To Dan & Eliza,
Peace Always,
Col. 3:15

His Peace
for
Your Life

Living Every Moment
in the Light of God's Promises

a devotional by

Neil Carmichael

PeacePoint Media
Charlotte

His Peace for Your Life
by Neil Carmichael

PeacePoint Media
info@peacepoint.com

International Standard Book Number: 978-0-615-99997-5

Printed in the United States of America

First Printing, May 2014

Second Printing, August 2014

Third Printing, March 2015

Publisher's Note:
All entries, prayers and poems were written by Neil Carmichael unless
otherwise noted.

Cover Design and page layout by Graeme Campbell.

Printed by CB Publishing & Design

This devotional was written for my son and daughter:

Aaron
The Adventurous Observer with an easygoing spirit
and a heart for God.

Bryn
The Compassionate Crusader with a resolute spirit
and a passion for Jesus.

And dedicated first

to Barbara, my wife, thank you for your love
throughout every moment of our story,

and second, to:

…all who run with perseverance the race marked out for us;
let the peace of Christ rule in your hearts.

CONTENTS

FOREWORD

Jesus' peace came to my life on April 7, 1979.

I had joined the Air Force four years earlier and was stationed at Randolph Air Force Base outside San Antonio, Texas. My wife Barbara worked as a bank teller. I was in the final months of a very successful enlistment, having received numerous awards including two Commendation Medals, the Meritorious Service Medal and Air Force-wide recognition for my contributions. At age 25, I had what many people spend a lifetime pursuing: influence, prestige and money. But I was not at peace.

Kay, one of Barbara's co-workers had, for several months, been inviting Barbara and me to attend a home Bible study. We found every excuse not to go. In early 1979, we attended a going-away party for another of Barbara's co-workers. Shortly after arriving, we realized we were the only ones there who were not part of the Bible study to which Kay had been inviting us.

The people were unlike any we had ever been around. They had a joy for life that was palpable. A genuine affection for one another that was foreign to us. And a spirit of love — and peace — we had never seen. They talked about Jesus as if they actually knew Him. It wasn't long before we were part of the Bible study.

Kay's husband, Larry, a commercial airline pilot, led the study. Every time Larry opened his Bible, the words came alive. The reality of God and His power seemed to jump off every page. Week-by-week, a stirring inside us grew and grew.

As we sat in Kay and Larry's apartment on the evening of April 7th listening as Larry shared yet another account from Jesus' life, I felt like I was about to burst with anticipation. "Larry," I interrupted, "For the first time in my life I believe that Jesus Christ is the Son of God, but I feel this emptiness. Like I have a big hole right here," pointing to the center of my chest. Immediately, Barbara said, "Me too!" At that moment, Barbara and I, holding hands, received Jesus Christ into our lives. Instantly, we were unburdened by the guilt of sin. God's indescribable love overwhelmed us. And the peace of Christ calmed our restless spirits.

The abiding presence of Jesus' peace lies at the heart of this devotional. Each selection affirms that God wants you to be at peace in Christ, living every moment in the light of His promises.

Neil Carmichael
2014

ACKNOWLEDGEMENTS

Acknowledging all who made this devotional possible, I begin with God the Father who gave me life; Jesus Christ, my Lord, who is the center of each daily entry; and His Holy Spirit for whatever insights and inspiration there may be on these pages.

I also gratefully acknowledge the following:

Tim Sellers for his love of Jesus, his friendship, and his devotion to helping people find peace with God and peace with others. Robert Whitlow for his writer's heart, generous advice and thoughtful guidance; it was his encouragement that turned a private writing exercise into this book.

The professors and staff at Reformed Theological Seminary Global, particularly Andy Peterson, Jim McAlhaney and Alice Hathaway, whose hearts for God and minds for truth contributed greatly to my intellectual and spiritual development.

Caroline McMillan Portillo for her diligent, thorough, and thoughtful editing; Janelle Young for her technical guidance and review in preparing the book for publication; Geoff Campbell for his friendship and gracious assistance; and all the saints (too many to list by name) I have been blessed to know along my spiritual journey who have enriched my life in countless ways.

Special acknowledgement goes to Larry and Kay Campbell for their faithfulness to the transforming power of salvation through Jesus Christ. Through their witness, Jesus' love, forgiveness, eternal life and peace came to Barbara and me. To them we are forever grateful.

And finally, Barbara my wife, whose love for me is only surpassed — as it should be — by her love for Jesus. A more perfect partner I could not imagine for life on this side of eternity.

Day 1

A Kingdom at Peace

...and the kingdom was at peace...
2 Chronicles 14:5

Sin tends to cause turmoil, not peace. This truth painfully manifested itself in my life in my early 40s. At the time I had a very active career. I was a church elder, a Cub Scout leader, an adult Sunday school teacher, a lecturer for a Wednesday Bible study, a husband to a wonderful wife, and a father to two great kids — a son, 9, and a daughter, 7.

One Friday I flew roundtrip from Charlotte to New York to meet my new boss. His message: I was going to face more demands and more pressure. The next day my wife was sidelined with a debilitating migraine. That meant I was on my own to carry a busy Saturday with the kids. By dinner time, I felt overwhelmed and started crying, finding it hard to stop as I stood at the stove. The uncontrollable sobbing returned on Sunday morning, before church. And after worship and two committee meetings, the tears returned yet again. But I had to head straight to the airport for a cross-country flight to Los Angeles.

As I struggled to regain my emotional equilibrium, I came across this business principle: "Your systems and procedures are perfectly designed to produce the results you are getting!"

My "systems and procedures" had successfully produced a world — my personal kingdom — that was not at peace.

King Asa did what was good and right in the eyes of the Lord his God.[1] He instituted reforms to rid the land of heathen deities and idolatrous practices. He commanded Judah to seek the Lord and obey His laws and commands. The "systems and procedures" instituted by Asa produced a kingdom at peace.

As a Christian, you must subject your personal kingdom to the operating principles of the Kingdom of God — the redemptive reign of Jesus Christ where everything is under His rule and authority. Living in the light of redemption leads to a kingdom at peace, not turmoil.

Father God, I lay on your altar all my aspirations so that I may do nothing out of selfish ambition or vain conceit. Make me ambitious to glorify and please you alone even if as a result I sink into obscurity, for I am not my own, I was bought at a price, purchased by the blood of Jesus. May my personal "kingdom" always be subject to the principles of your Kingdom so it will always be a kingdom at peace.

DAY 2

The Desire for Peace

Seek peace and pursue it.
Psalm 34:14

PEACE IS SECOND ONLY TO LOVE as the condition most sought after by the human heart. This is because a heart at peace gives life to the body.[1] Inherently knowing this, your heart makes peace an object of its desire.

We desire what we believe will bring satisfaction or enjoyment. It may be something once possessed and then lost, or something you never had. The state of being at peace, as a condition of the human heart, falls in the first category.

Adam and Eve were at peace in paradise because of their position in relation to God. Nothing separated them from Him. They lost their peace because of their disobedience. Eve allowed herself to be deceived by Satan and Adam rejected God's command to not eat of the tree of the knowledge of good and evil. As a consequence, their position in relation to God changed.

When God asked Adam after he'd sinned, "Where are you?" the reference was to position, not location. God was asking, "Now that you have chosen to be autonomous, where does that leave you in relation to me?"

The contrast between humanity's relation to God in its original state of dependence and its relation to God in its fallen state of autonomy is striking: life exchanged for death, pleasure exchanged for pain, abundance for want, honesty for deception, harmony for discord — the veritable world of miseries is painfully extensive.

That's why there is a universal discontent with this state of affairs; one that is so stinging it creates in each of us a desire for what was lost when humanity became estranged from God: peace.

Is your heart at peace? If so, rejoice in Jesus' gift to you. If not, let today be the day you seek peace and pursue it.

Father God, you reached out and touched my life when my soul was dark and lost. Thank you for giving me Jesus' love and peace, the most sought-after desires of my heart.

DAY 3

The Source of Peace

For he himself is our peace.
Ephesians 2:14

How often do you reflect on the things in your life for which Jesus is the source? When Jesus was on his way to heal the 12-year-old daughter of Jairus, a synagogue ruler, the crowd around him was so great it almost crushed him. When a woman in the crowd touched the edge of his cloak, Jesus said, "Someone touched me; I know that power has gone out from me." The woman and the crowd learned an astonishing truth: Jesus is the source of a power that brings healing to peoples' lives.

Have you recently contemplated Jesus as the source of all things?[1] Being co-eternal with and of the same essence as God the Father, He is Creator of the universe and the source of your very life.

When did you last meditate on Jesus as the source of your redemption and salvation? Being fully God and fully man, Jesus alone, by His death, is the atoning sacrifice for your sins, making Him your Lord and Savior. How long has it been since you reflected on the fact that Jesus — resurrected and glorified — is the source of your eternal life? And when did you last ponder that, because of His being and power, Jesus is the source of every provision you need?

Reflect on these truths often and you'll be filled with an overwhelming sense of the peace, which is your birthright as a child of God. But Jesus does more than bring peace. He is the sole source of true peace   not just because of what He did, but because of who He is. He himself is your peace.

Lord Jesus, Son of God, by you and for you all things were created, whether visible or invisible. All the fullness of the Father dwells in you, and through you, He is reconciling to himself all creation, including my life. You are my source of peace through your blood that was shed on the cross.

When I look around my world and see,
All you have provided me;
All cares and worries I can release;
Knowing you are my source of peace.

DAY 4

Peace of Mind

...But we have the mind of Christ.
1 Corinthians 2:16

DID YOU BEGIN YOUR MORNING by chasing thoughts inside your head? Before your feet hit the floor, did any peace of mind you enjoyed while sleeping quickly vanish? Even at night, your mind often finds no rest, as unwelcome thieves with names like Worry, Stress, Busyness, Envy, Greed, Guilt, Lust, Heartbreak, Fear and Doubt invade your thoughts. Peace of mind eludes you. Like the psalmist, you cry out wearily, "How long must I wrestle with my thoughts?"[1]

Your mind is the fountain from which your human consciousness flows, bringing with it the thoughts, perceptions, images, emotions, will and memories that influence your mental and physical behavior. In short: It's an active place, and yet longs to be at peace.

Paradoxically, peace of mind is not a product of the mind. The human mind, tainted by sin, cannot be the source of its own peace. The source of peace must be external.

The Apostle Paul captures these truths when he says, "The mind of sinful man is death, but the mind controlled by the Spirit is life and peace."[2] For the Christian, peace of mind is possible thanks to the indwelling presence of the Holy Spirit. No longer compelled to wrestle only with its own thoughts, your mind can be free to contemplate what is true, noble, right, pure, lovely, admirable, excellent and praiseworthy[3] because you have the mind of Christ. When peace of mind eludes you, yield your thought life to the transforming power of Jesus' mind.

Jesus, be Lord over my mind, for it is where I live and it is the battleground of the Enemy. Guard my mind against deceitful desires and make me aware of Satan's schemes, so that I can take my stand against them and not be outwitted. Renew my mind so every thought is brought captive to you, bound to contemplate what is true, noble, right, pure, lovely, admirable, excellent and praiseworthy. Grant me peace of mind because I have the mind of Christ.

DAY 5

Enmity

And I will put enmity between you and the woman,
and between your offspring and hers; he will crush
your head, and you will strike his heel."
Genesis 3:15

A POPULAR BUMPER STICKER ENCOURAGES PEOPLE to "visualize world peace." It's a nice sentiment, but the advocates of world peace are unaware of a stark reality: God has ordained, in this present age, world enmity, not world peace.

Enmity is a state of affairs characterized by severe hatred and desire for murder. Biblically, it is a tragic consequence of The Fall. God told Adam, Eve and the serpent, Satan, that from that point forward the stream of humanity would be divided by enmity. Those who by the corruption of Satan are spiritually dead will incessantly oppose those who — by the redemptive acts of God culminating in the atonement of Jesus Christ — are spiritually alive. This intense opposition is the direct spiritual cause of the world's conflicts, small and epic.

You, too, can be plagued by your own thoughts of enmity. You may want to think that you're not capable of such a dark and insidious emotion, but you are. The original sin, which we are infected with, predisposes each of us to declare, "I am my own God." And as evident in the life of King David, that false belief has the potential to produce in us an enmity toward people who stand in the way of our getting what we want.[1]

As a Christian, you don't need to be dismayed by enmity and its menacing effects because God is sovereign and Jesus has overcome the world.[2] So when others oppose you, let the peace of Christ rather than enmity rule in your heart.[3]

Heavenly Father, protect my heart from enmity. May the peace of Christ and His love and mercies always rule my interactions with others. And when I consider the condition of this fallen world, help me to always find peace knowing that your sovereign hand will prevail.

DAY 6

Love

Do you truly love…?
John 21:16

"**D**O YOU LOVE AS I LOVE?" That's the question Jesus asks Peter on the shoreline.[1] Twice, Jesus — using the Greek word *agape* — asks Peter, "Do you truly love me?" And both times, Peter replies, "You know I love you," using the word *philo*. Jesus is asking Peter if he loves Him with the highest form of love, one that's selfless and unconditional (agape). Peter confesses that his love for Jesus is of a lesser degree, one simply of tender affection (philo). Jesus, when asking a third time, uses the word philo rather than agape.

Peter understands the impact of the word change, knowing, with sadness, that he can't love as Jesus loves. Why? He can't follow the "way of love"[2] because he does not yet have the Holy Spirit. Without the indwelling presence of the Holy Spirit, humanity can't express the agape love of God revealed in Jesus.

Agape love is patient and kind. It's not envious, boastful or proud. It's not rude, self-seeking or easily angered. It keeps no record of wrongs, does not delight in evil and rejoices in what's true. It always protects, always trusts, always hopes and never gives up.[3]

In Christ Jesus, the only thing that counts is faith expressing itself through love.[4] And Jesus' desire for you, as it was for Peter, is that you can be the kind of person from whom agape love flows naturally; the kind of person who is patient and kind, and all the other facets of unconditional love. As a Christian, the inner dimensions of your soul have been transformed by the Holy Spirit, and that means you are indeed that kind of person.

Follow the way of love, and the presence of God's peace will never diminish.

Lord Jesus, you came in love so that people could know your Father. The love that brought you into the world was altogether foreign — unconditional, sacrificial, intentional, and selfless. It's a bit foreign still, but may it continue to transform my heart so I can love others — no matter who they are or how different from me they may be — with the same love with which you love me. And as I follow the way of your love, may its attending peace never diminish.

DAY 7

Only Dimly

For now we see in a mirror dimly...
Now I know in part; then I shall know fully...
1 Corinthians 13:12[1]

THE CLEAREST EXPRESSION OF UNCONDITIONAL LOVE in all of literature is found in the Apostle Paul's first letter to the Christians at the church in Corinth.[2] Yet the picture Paul paints is not a complete one. Paul himself acknowledges this, saying "For now, we see (love) in a mirror dimly."

By using the word "dimly," Paul is saying that we can see the truth, but our sin keeps us from seeing it in perfect clarity.

Sin has the power to obscure our knowledge of God and distort His truths. We can only see part of the picture, and yet we talk and act as if we clearly see the whole. Paul knew better. He knew that as clear as his vision of God's love was, he was incapable of seeing the fullness of it in this life. But he was not discouraged. For Paul, seeing "dimly" did not make the unconditional love of God any less real.

This is also true of the peace Jesus gives to you. As deeply as you can experience His peace now — a peace that passes all understanding[3] — it's still but a reflection of the peace you will experience in the new heaven and earth that are yet to come.[4]

So don't be discouraged when Jesus' peace appears dim to you. Remember that it's sin that causes you to experience the ebb and flow of His peace; the peace of Christ is not actually dim.

On your Spirit within I do rely
For discerning your truths from whim;
So comfort me, Lord, when your truths are obscured
And the peace of Christ appears dim.

DAY 8

At Peace with Doubt

Then Jesus said to Thomas, "Put your finger here; see my
hands. Reach out your hand and put it into my side.
Stop doubting and believe."
John 20:27

Immediately Jesus reached out his hand and caught Peter.
"You of little faith," he said, "why did you doubt?"
Matthew 14:31

ENTERING SEMINARY JUST A FEW WEEKS SHY of my
50th birthday, I had what most Christians would
characterize as a mature faith. Nonetheless, there
were brief moments during my studies that caused me
to question and occasionally doubt the truth of a
particular doctrine, tradition or historical account.
This eventually brought me to a crossroad, a moment

— somewhere between pondering the esoteric musings presented in the history of philosophy and wrestling with the arcane precepts of church dogmatics — when I thought: Christianity is either true or it's not.

The Apostles Peter and Thomas and evangelist Billy Graham had similar pivotal moments. At one time in his life, Dr. Graham struggled with believing the Bible is the authoritative Word of God. He began to doubt, struggling over the question of the integrity of the Word of God.[1] Likewise, Peter began to sink when he doubted Jesus' ability to sustain him as he walked toward him on the Sea of Galilee. And Thomas doubted his fellow disciples when they reported that Jesus was alive, having appeared to them after His resurrection.

"Doubt is but another element of faith," St. Augustine said. Just when you think you're at peace with what you believe, doubt often creeps in. But just like the irritation of a foreign substance creates a pearl inside an oyster, the irritation of doubt can promote spiritual growth and maturity inside of you.

Peter, Thomas, Billy Graham and I didn't have all our questions answered, but we each navigated a major crossroad and continued our Christian journey at peace with doubt.

I have doubts, Lord Jesus, but I take comfort in knowing they are necessary to my spiritual growth. As I wrestle with each one, I pray to be like Abraham who did not waver through unbelief, but was strengthened in his faith and gave glory to God. And when I encounter questions that have no satisfactory answers, I ask that I may continue my journey with you at peace with my doubt.

DAY 9

At Peace with Mystery

How...unfathomable His ways!
Romans 11:34

YOUR WESTERN MIND VALUES MASTERY over mystery. It wants questions answered and contradictions resolved. It applies Aristotelian and Socratic models of thinking — and their emphasis on the empirical, the scientific, and the practical — to virtually all areas of your life. It insists on logical, systematic, well-organized, and well-reasoned investigation and analysis. It is uncomfortable with inconsistency or contradiction. It is not at peace with mystery, particularly of the theological kind.

How deep is your insight into the three most enduring theological mysteries of the Christian faith — the doctrine of the Trinity, the problem of evil, and the relationship between individual free will and God's sovereignty? These regularly serve up very difficult spiritual challenges for Western Christians.

What is God like that He can be three Persons in one — All doing what each does, each doing what all do, and all living in you as each lives in the others?[1] Where is justice when the righteous get what the wicked deserve and the wicked get what the righteous deserve?[2] How is it that in your heart, you plan your course, but the Lord determines your steps?[3]

Nothing is a mystery to God. He's omniscient — never curious, bewildered, perplexed or confused. He knows, understands and comprehends all things perfectly.

Mystery surrounding the things of God is necessary to faith. It is essential that certain things concerning God transcend your understanding. Applying rational, logical, analytical thought processes to your investigation of them will bring little insight. You should think theologically because you are a theist. Thinking theologically will not solve the mysteries of God, but it will bring you closer to being at peace with them.

Father, God Almighty, who is there in heaven or on earth who can do the deeds and mighty works you do? You are exalted over all the nations and your glory is above the heavens. You know the beginning from the end. Where was I when you laid the foundations of the earth? It is you who made me, not the other way around. I can neither probe your limits nor fathom your mysteries. In your mercy grant me peace in all I do not understand.

DAY 10

At Peace with Unanswered Prayer

...sorrowful, yet always rejoicing...
2 Corinthians 6:10

IT WAS HER LIFE'S "GREAT SADNESS;" a spiritually devastating period of unanswered prayer. Do you hear me? Did I hear you? Did I miss something? Do you really care? Will I ever be at peace with this? These were among my wife's anguished cries — for days, weeks, months, and years.

We can expect crushing disappointment if we put our faith in the things of this world. But as Christians, we believe — and expect — that such disappointment should not befall us when our faith is placed in the One who made us, whose compassion is endless and love unconditional. And yet, many Christians have struggled with and been spiritually wounded by unanswered prayer.

Next to the existence of evil — what theologians call "theodicy" — unanswered prayer can be the most vexing mystery. It's hard to reconcile a holy and just God with the existence of evil. And when faced with unanswered prayer, it can be difficult for a Christian to reconcile how a loving and compassionate God could appear so indifferent. The more significant the request — and the longer the prayer goes unanswered — the more crushing God's apparent indifference is, especially when the request appears to be within His will as revealed in Scripture.

Supporters of those enduring the struggle can offer consolation but no satisfying answer. God alone has the answer. This presented a nettlesome paradox for my wife: The only way to keep life uncrushed in the presence of unanswered prayer was to steadfastly trust the One whom she held, in some measure, responsible for the disappointment. But it was only by trusting that she, like the Apostle Paul, could be sorrowful yet always rejoicing because the object of her faith knows all things perfectly. Trusting God makes it possible to be at peace with unanswered prayer.

I know it's OK to be impatient. I know it's OK to be frustrated. I even know, Father God, it's OK to be mad at you. But knowing these things is little consolation when I struggle with unanswered prayer. Much of what I know to be true — like knowing you hear the righteous when they cry out to you and knowing you are close to the brokenhearted — doesn't seem to be true. Please help me discern your sovereign hand in the circumstances and fix my eyes on eternal realities, so I can be at peace when experiencing unanswered prayer.

DAY 11

Peace in Serving Others

Each one should use whatever gift he has received
to serve others, faithfully administering
God's grace in its various forms.
1 Peter 4:10

I ONCE HEARD A STORY ABOUT General William Booth, the founder of the Salvation Army, which illustrates his ministry efforts as well as the essence of Jesus' ministry.

Around 1900, General Booth was preparing to send his annual Christmas greeting to all Salvation Army troops serving throughout the world. He planned to send the message by telegraph, and the companies charged by the word. Because of financial constraints,

Booth had to send a short message. In fact, his was a single word: "Others!"

Booth recognized that we are most like Jesus when we are serving others. Those who have never lost themselves in the service of others have been deprived of one of life's greatest blessings.

"Others" are at the heart of the gospel. The Son of Man did not come to be served, but to serve.[1] "Whoever wants to become great among you must be your servant," Jesus said, "and whoever wants to be first must be slave of all."[2]

Oswald Chambers expressed Jesus' urging this way: "In sanctification, the one who has been born again deliberately gives up his right to himself to Jesus Christ, and identifies himself entirely with God's ministry to others."[3] Without question, we are to use our God-given gifts to serve others.[4]

When you set out to make the day better for someone else — whether giving an encouraging word or visit, praying for a friend or stranger, or volunteering for the benefit of someone other than yourself — you will sleep well at night with both your heart and mind at peace.

Lord, help me live from day to day,
In such a self-forgetful way;
That even when I kneel to pray,
My prayer shall be for – Others.

Others, Lord, yes others,
Let this my motto be,
Help me to live for others,
That I may live like Thee.

~ From the hymn "Others" by Charles D. Meigs

DAY 12

Peace through Your Giftedness

We have different gifts, according to the grace given us.
Romans 12:6

My son, Aaron, was 8 years old when he declared, "Weather is my life!" Today he is a meteorologist. Early in life he was aware of one area of his giftedness.

Giftedness is the sum of all the abilities God has given you, and He intends to use them to glorify Himself and demonstrate his love for people. Each gift God endowed you with is on loan, and should be cultivated, explored and exercised. They are essential to your calling, your purpose, and your assignments from God.

Your calling is to love the Lord your God with all your heart, soul, mind and strength, and to love your neighbor as yourself.[1] Your purpose is where your love for God intersects with the needs of people. Your assignments are what God gives you to do for a season within your calling.[2] And when your calling, purpose and assignments converge, your giftedness opens pathways for you to have influence.

Your influence flows from who you are and how you relate to other people, what you know and how you use that knowledge, and what gifts you possess and how skillfully you exercise them. As I approached graduating from seminary in my mid-50s, a friend posed the very penetrating question, "In light of the gifts God has given you, who do you want to influence?"

How would you answer that question?

Everyone's giftedness is different – and powerful. But nobody made a greater mistake than he who did nothing because he thought little of his giftedness. Use your gifts without any hesitation or anxiety; in this way you will enjoy peace with God and recognize His limitless generosity towards you.[3]

Lord Jesus, I thank you for my giftedness and the peace it brings from using it for your glory. I pray that others will see you through the gifts and talents you have given me. As the tool is at the mercy of the craftsman and the pen yields to the impulses of the writer, take me in your hands today and use me as an instrument of your will.

DAY 13

Pain, Suffering, Sorrow and Peace

He will wipe every tear from their eyes…
Revelation 21:4

W E HAVE A VERY SMALL and incomplete picture of reality, viewing times of pain, suffering and sorrow as some of life's worst moments. And we exacerbate the feeling when we believe that our Heavenly Father has betrayed us or isn't as trustworthy as we'd thought. In our misery, we judge Him — finding God guilty of actions we determine to be unworthy of His divine character. Yet, we fail to remember that it was humanity that ushered evil into this world.

So God isn't the author or agent of pain, suffering and sorrow. The notion that He is only leads to false perceptions about Him. That God does not always restrain evil is bewildering. That He is sovereign over evil is mystifying. That He permitted evil to come into the life of His beloved Son Jesus is unimaginable; and yet it also is wonderfully consoling. Through Jesus' life and death, God Himself became intimately acquainted with our misery.

Because God is sovereign, He brings into your life only those things that are in accord with His will for you.[1] Your independence and autonomy are uncomfortable with this. You would rather be the ultimate decider of the events that shape your destiny. But the reality is different. God's purposes will stand, and He will do what He pleases.[2]

When our broken world causes pain, suffering, and sorrow to come to you, remember that God's purpose is to redeem these experiences, just as He did in Jesus' life. Trust Him to bring healing out of pain, comfort out of suffering, joy out of sorrow and peace to your soul.

Pain, suffering and sorrow are unwelcome visitors. Have mercy upon me, Father God, so that their visits in my life are few. And when they do come, I pray you will work healing out of pain, comfort out of suffering, joy out of sorrow, and bring peace to my soul. With you weeping may remain for a night, but rejoicing comes in the morning. I look forward with joyful anticipation to the day when you will wipe every tear, and there will be no more death, mourning, crying or pain.

DAY 14

Peace Lost

Though the mountains be shaken and the hills be removed,
yet my unfailing love for you will not be shaken nor my
covenant of peace be removed," says the Lord,
who has compassion on you.
Isaiah 54:10

LIFE IN A FALLEN WORLD COMES WITH CURVEBALLS. My mom had not been feeling well, so my dad took her to the hospital. She died three days later. Quite suddenly, the woman who had nursed my cuts and bruises, taught me manners and tirelessly enriched my life in countless ways was, all too soon, gone.

Seven years later, Janet, a dear friend, called. The diagnosis: lung cancer. She died less than a year later.

Janet was the epitome of grace, a teacher in her prime who touched the lives of hundreds of kids and was the heart and soul of our decade-old adult Sunday school class. And now she was gone — again, all too soon.

These curveballs were emotionally and spiritually traumatic. My peace instantly vaporized like still water seared by a flash of intense heat.

Our Heavenly Father is also familiar with curveballs. This is comforting. He experienced Satan's rebellion in heaven and Adam's and Eve's fall from grace on earth. The impact of these events on Him was unbelievably painful. Unlike us, however, He sees curveballs coming and, being God, He suffers no loss of peace.

When life's curveballs conspire against you and you experience a loss of peace, you are at the mercy of your faith — its depth and steadfastness or its shallowness and uncertainly. If your faith is in your faith, it will tend toward the shallow, uncertain end of the spiritual pool and peace will be elusive. If it is in the One who created you — in whom you live and move and have your being[1] — your faith will tend toward deep and steadfast spiritual waters. And His peace, though momentarily lost, will, without fail, return to you.

O Lord, my Rock and my Redeemer, you heal the brokenhearted and bind up their wounds. You give strength to the weary and your compassion comforts them in their suffering and distress. Your righteous right hand upholds those who are dismayed. My consolation when peace is momentarily lost is that I have set you always before me. You are the Rock on which I stand. I may be disheartened, but I will not be shaken.

Day 15

At Peace with Death

Those who walk uprightly enter into peace;
they find rest as they lie in death.
Isaiah 57:2

Such great and wonderful things would never have
been done for us by God, if the life of the soul
were to end with the death of the body.
St. Augustine[1]

BODY AND SOUL WERE NEVER MEANT to be separated. When viewing someone who has passed away at funerals, I am always struck by this thought: there's nothing natural about "natural death."

It is the unnatural character of death that makes it so emotionally painful and the prospect of the body separating from the soul so unsettling. At the core of our being we know it's not God's intent for death to be a part of life. It is a consequence of disobedience.

After eating from the tree of the knowledge of good and evil, Adam and Eve were denied the prospect of living forever — prohibited by God from eating from the tree of life.[2] The repetition of the lament, "then he died," in the pages of Genesis punctuates the depth of the tragedy from which death springs. It echoes across human history like a mournful refrain from God's broken heart, grief-stricken that it must be this way.

And yet, in a world marred by sin and all its devastating consequences, living forever would be, for humanity, hell on earth. It's difficult to comprehend, but physical death is an act of God's mercy.

When death comes to those who don't know Christ, eternity is grim. But when death comes to Christians, we should do as James says and "count it all joy," for

Scripture declares that the day of death is better than the day of birth.[3] At physical death, the Christian immediately enters Jesus' presence and the glorious heavenly existence of happiness that continues until the final resurrection, Christ's Second Coming, when the soul is united with a glorified body. Then we will live forever on the new earth, enjoying its unfathomable beauty and tranquility. Death has lost its sting![4] So what reason do we have to be at anything but peace with it?

You saved me Jesus, my sin to kill,
Called to serve your sovereign will;
By your Spirit stirred or still,
My life has brought you glory.

Sanctified and redeemed,
no longer bound but free,
Come the day I breathe my last,
at peace with death I'll be.

DAY 16

The Bond of Peace

*Make every effort to keep the unity of the Spirit
through the bond of peace.*
Ephesians 4:3

"**Y**OU'RE FIRED!"

The words weren't unexpected. Turned out I possessed a character trait fatal to sales professionals: I hated searching for new clients. Immediately, I called to share the grim news with my wife, Barbara, who was still at work. Standing by her desk was Bill, a dear friend who had, providentially, stopped by her office. Sensing all was not well, he asked her what was wrong. Barbara relayed the news. His reply: "Tell Neil to meet me in 20 minutes at San Remo's."

It was a restaurant where guys from church regularly ate breakfast together, and I arrived to find Bill and Pastor Olson. They spent the next two hours of their lives comforting and encouraging me. I still get misty-eyed every time I share this story.

Bill and Pastor Olson are two members of a special group that has been with me and my family as the stream of life has carried us along. Some of the group have been in the stream with us for decades; others joined more recently. And some, like Bill, are now with Jesus.

As a group, we've experienced smooth currents that bring blessings and currents as turbulent as whitewater rapids that bring heartache. (Parenting falls into both categories!) This cherished group has a name: fellow Christians. We are brothers and sisters in Christ, and the Holy Spirit has graciously brought us into one another's lives to challenge, encourage, support — and most importantly — love one another.

Cultivating Christian fellowship is indispensible to your spiritual well-being.[1]   This fellowship has a strength and character that's different from that of your secular friendships.   The unique character of Christian fellowship comes from having as its center the Person and work of Jesus Christ rather than worldly interests and pursuits.   Its unique strength is the bond of peace[2] forged by loving one another as Jesus loves us.

Help me today, Lord, to encourage other people in their walk with you.   Please give me the eyes to see their need, the ears to hear their requests and the heart to truly care for them.   May their life and my life be enriched by the bond of peace forged by the love of Jesus we have for one another.

DAY 17

Peace on the Lighter Side

...a time to laugh...
Ecclesiastes 3:4

AFTER BEING SICK FOR THREE DAYS, my wife ventured downstairs for dinner, only to hear our son, 9 years old at the time, blurt out: "Gee, mom, if you had bolts coming out of your neck you would look just like Frankenstein's wife!" To this day, it's still one of our family's best laughs.

Humor is so important to our well-being that there's an area of psychology dedicated to studying how laughter affects people. It's called gelotology (not to be confused with jellotology, the study of the inexplicable popularity of artificially enhanced gelatinous animal collagen).

Everyone has favorite jokes that trigger a good laugh even if you've heard it countless times. Here's one of my favorites:

> Pastor Turner decided to play hooky one Sunday. After calling in sick, he headed out to the golf course. Observing the pastor's behavior, St. Peter said to God, "I'm appalled Pastor Turner would do such a thing."
>
> Just then, the pastor hit a hole-in-one. St. Peter was outraged and complained to God, "Instead of punishing him, why did you reward him with a hole-in-one?!"
>
> God smiled and replied, "Who's he going to tell?"

And here's another:

> A priest, an evangelist, and a rabbi each go into the woods to find a bear to convert to see who's best at his job. Meeting two hours later the priest begins: "Found a bear, read from the Catechism, sprinkled him with holy water. Next week is his

First Communion." The evangelist then says: "Found a bear, preached God's holy word and baptized him." Then they both look at the rabbi, with a bloody body and shredded clothes. "Looking back," he says, "maybe I shouldn't have started with circumcision."

Humor, a gift from God, can be a saving grace, with the power to overcome difficulties, dissipate disappointment and relieve pain.[1]   Laugh often and enjoy peace on the lighter side.

*A heart at peace gives life to the body and a
happy heart makes the face cheerful.
Lord, make me laugh today.*

Day 18

Impediments to Peace

Watch out for…obstacles in your way that are contrary
to the teaching you have learned.
Romans 16:17

WHEN READING JESUS' PENETRATING Sermon on the Mount,[1] you see that He addresses a number of impediments to your having His peace in your life, including: doing "acts of righteousness" in public, offering up "babbling" prayers, refusing to forgive, storing up treasure on earth, looking at things that allow darkness to enter your body, trying to serve two masters, worrying, judging, being indiscriminate, failing to ask of God, failing to treat others as you like to be treated, listening to false teachers, failing to build your life on the rock-solid foundation of Jesus' words.

However, if you see the Sermon on the Mount as a collection of independent, legalistic dos and don'ts, they will impede your ability to experience Jesus' peace. Jesus is not here giving laws. His overarching message in the Sermon is to convey the kingdom reality that true acts of righteousness — prayer, forgiveness, your storing up treasure in heaven, and the others — are matters of the heart, not a commitment to obeying a set of laws.

Jesus Christ is your peace just as much as He is your Savior. When you entered the kingdom of God as one born again of the Spirit,[2] you received as your birthright both salvation and peace. Satan will entice you to doubt this. His means are counterfeits to the peace Jesus alone provides. Be on your guard against his counterfeit peace. You cannot fully experience the peace that comes through Jesus while having an ambition for power or prestige, or desiring fame, money or material possessions.

But if you first desire an intimate relationship with Jesus and the things of His kingdom, then God will give you what you need.[3] Seek Jesus first and all the rest will magnify His peace in your life, not impede it.

Come, Holy Spirit, protect my heart and soul so they are never deceived by Satan's counterfeit instruction. Guide my practice of the spiritual disciplines, as found in Jesus' teachings, in such a way that they remain sincere expressions of my renewed heart and never decline into legalistic dos and don'ts. For I know those would impede my growth in the grace of Jesus Christ and His peace in my life.

DAY 19

The Knowledge of God

*For since the creation of the world God's invisible qualities
— his eternal power and divine nature — have been clearly
seen, being understood from what has been made, so that
men are without excuse.*

Romans 1:20

TWENTIETH CENTURY THEOLOGIAN A.W. Tozer said,
"What enters our mind when we think about God is
the most important thing about us."[1] A lofty concept
of God is so necessary to your being at peace that
when it declines in any measure, your peace declines
with it.

There's a school of thought that says God, if He exists,
is so different and remote from Man that we have no
real concept of Him. He is, in fact, unknowable.

Therefore, He does not communicate with us, we owe Him nothing, and we humans are, practically speaking, our own gods, living autonomous lives of moral relativism.

As a Christian, however, you know the error in this school of thought. Yes, God is wholly other. In His being He is unlike anything in Creation. And yet, in spite of this transcendence, God has chosen not to be wholly hidden. He has condescended to reveal Himself to us; first in His creation, second in His Word, and ultimately through Jesus in the Incarnation.

So what enters your mind when you think of Him? Is God a stern overlord, quick to punish at the slightest infraction of His rules, or a grandfatherly figure so all-loving that He wouldn't intentionally condemn anyone to hell? Is God a nearly all-powerful being who needs your help to get His work done? Or is He the Creator who oversees the big picture, but leaves you to manage the details?

Ask the Holy Spirit to cultivate in you a profound understanding of God's awesome character: His self-existence and self-sufficiency; His eternality, immutability, and wisdom; His omniscience, omnipotence and omnipresence; His faithfulness, goodness, justice, mercy, grace, love, holiness and sovereignty. There is peace in knowing God as He has truly revealed Himself.

Show yourself to me, O God,
but only what you dare,
Revealing your full Self to me
is more than I could bear.
I know you'll leave me wanting,
and that's as it should be,
For what need would I have then of faith,
if I knew all of Thee.

Help me somehow comprehend
your mercy, love and grace,
But keep me always ever-awed,
by your command of time and space.
Trembling at your mighty power,
and all Creation it has spun,
I yet have peace in knowing you,
as revealed in God the Son.

DAY 20

Settle Matters Quickly

Settle matters quickly with your adversary…
Matthew 5:25

BY THE TIME I WAS ASKED TO MEDIATE a multi-million dollar controversy, the adversaries — four ministry partners with a business relationship — had been at odds for eight years! My involvement marked their 16th attempt to resolve the controversy's business issues and reconcile the damage to their relationships. The experience was one of the most challenging assignments of my professional career.

Disputes and conflicts — whether with colleagues, family or friends — require that those involved incur certain "transactional costs" if they want closure, and each transactional cost has the potential to negatively impact everyone involved. This is precisely why Jesus, in His Sermon on the Mount, exhorts His listeners to "settle matters quickly."

Transactional costs come in the form of time, money, and emotional capital.

Time: Pulitzer Prize winning writer Carl Sandburg describes it as the coin of your life. "It is the only coin you have, and only you can determine how it will be spent," he says. "Be careful lest you let others spend it for you."[1] Disputes and conflicts will spend it for you.

Money: The financial cost of disputes and conflicts can be enormous, particularly if a lawsuit is involved.

Emotional Capital: When you invest emotions in the positive, you are energized, but when you spend them on the negative, you are demoralized. And that's why navigating disputes and conflicts — no matter how constructive the eventual outcome may be — requires an expenditure of emotional capital that always takes a negative toll.

In the controversy I mediated, the partners' expenditures of time and emotion were particularly devastating, but would have been much less so had they settled matters quickly. Eventually, they did reach a mutually acceptable mediated outcome. Their disputes were resolved. Their relationships reconciled. God was glorified. Peace was found.

Lord, you have set before me all spiritual principles and social conventions necessary to manage my affairs in ways that honor you. Your Word, your Spirit, and your Son provide all the instruction, guidance and wisdom I need so my words and actions do not spark controversies; but when controversies do come my way, I commit to making peace by settling them quickly in ways that glorify you.

DAY 21

Elements of True Peace

Therefore, since we have been justified through faith,
we have peace with God through our Lord Jesus Christ.
Romans 5:1

FOUR ELEMENTS OF THE CHRISTIAN LIFE — salvation, grace, sanctification and discipleship — are indispensable for us to be able to reflect the peace we have in Christ.

The regeneration of salvation, explains how a person who was once dead in trespasses and sins, whose mind was at enmity with God, and who could not naturally do that which is well-pleasing to God can experience peace with God, peace with himself, and peace with others.

Grace is God's selecting for Himself a people from the ranks of imperfect and rebellious humanity. There is nothing meritorious within the chosen that warrants their selection. The basis of selection is God's pleasure alone. The significance of being at peace through grace is this: A people saved from eternal separation from God through no effort of their own, and knowing that there is nothing in and of themselves that makes them even remotely worthy of being saved, are at peace with God. They should, therefore, unhesitatingly exhibit to others the grace and peace they themselves have so freely received.

Sanctification is the process of eliminating all of one's sin and transforming the soul into the image of God's own Son. Although the process of sanctification isn't completed this side of eternity, it brings peace to the soul in the midst of a fallen world.

Discipleship with Jesus involves far more than being just a follower of His; it means we must give nothing less than our complete personal commitment to Him and His message. Jesus' disciples are those who have received the life, fellowship and attending peace of the Kingdom of God.

Father God, Lord Jesus, Holy Spirit, I could never adequately express my gratitude for all you have done and continue to do for me. You saved me, even though I've done nothing to merit it. You extended me grace for an abundant life I don't deserve. You began the good work of sanctifying me, knowing it will not be brought to completion unless I continually rely on you. And you called me to follow you with complete personal commitment, though my heart is prone to wander. I am forever grateful for these elements of your life in mine and the true peace they bring.

DAY 22

A Fruit of the Spirit

But the fruit of the Spirit is...peace...
Galatians 5:22

YOU MAY HAVE NOTICED that trying to exhibit the fruit of the Spirit in your daily life is different than letting the fruit of the Spirit flow through you — just as there is a difference between trying to live in the Spirit of Jesus and letting the Spirit of Jesus live in you.   In each instance, the former is a matter of striving; the latter a matter of yielding.

Botanists group fruit into several different categories, one of which is known as "multiple fruit." A multiple fruit is formed from a cluster of flowers, and each individual flower produces a separate fruit. Together, they mature into a single mass.

This is strikingly similar to the way the fruit of the Spirit works, as the Apostle Paul described it to the Christians in Galatia.[1] Like a multiple fruit, the fruit of the Spirit contains its own cluster of flowers — love, joy, peace, patience, kindness, goodness, faithfulness, gentleness and self-control. When cultivated, they mature into a single mass: the Holy Spirit's character in you.

Like fruit, the Spirit's peace and its companion flowers are sweet. And by yielding to it and letting it flow through you, the Spirit produces countless pleasant effects that counter the acts of the sinful nature, such as hatred, discord, rage, dissension and factions.[2] The Spirit's peace brings resolution to disputes and reconciliation to broken relationships, whether between family, friends, or coworkers — and particularly between fellow Christians.

Thank you, Father, for the gift of the Holy Spirit — the one who generates life and animates souls, who overcomes and destroys the power of sin so the human heart can bear His fruit, who helps the Church grow and helps me navigate life's challenges and stay faithful. You've called me to love you and love others, and I thank you, Holy Spirit, for subduing my sinful nature, so my life can bear and share your fruit of peace.

DAY 23

Forgiveness and Peace

*Forgive as the Lord forgave you. And over all these virtues
put on love, which binds them all together in perfect unity.
Let the peace of Christ rule in your hearts.
Colossians 3:13-15*

CORRIE TEN BOOM SPENT SEVERAL MONTHS near the
end of World War II in a Nazi concentration camp.
Her sister, Betsie, died there. The indignities and
humiliation they suffered were unimaginable. Two
years later, she traveled to Munich from her native
Holland to share a simple yet profound message: God
forgives. "It was the truth they needed most to hear in
that bitter, bombed-out land," she said.[1]

At the conclusion of her talk in a church basement, Corrie, to her surprise, came face to face with one of her former captors. "My blood seemed to freeze," she said. The man told her he had become a Christian and, extending his hand, asked for her forgiveness.

Coldness clutched her heart. But Corrie remembered that Jesus said if we don't forgive others their sins, God will not forgive ours.[2] She remembered that forgiveness is not an emotion, but an act of the will. She reminded herself that forgiveness does not excuse anything and that those who forgive can rebuild their lives; those who do not remain invalids. And finally, she remembered that without forgiveness, there is no peace.

We are to forgive just as Jesus forgave us.[3] The nature of this forgiveness is divine, not human, and it flows from us when we let the peace of Christ rule in our hearts.[4] We forgive, but not without help.

"Help!" Corrie prayed silently to God. "I can lift my hand. I can do that much. You supply the feeling." As she stretched out her hand, the current started in her shoulder, raced down her arm and sprang into their joined hands. Warmth flooded her whole being. "I forgive you, brother!" She cried. "With all my heart!"

To experience God's forgiveness, and at the same time be unforgiving toward another, is to deny Jesus and forfeit His peace.

Your divine forgiveness is altogether unfathomable. By it you, the only righteous judge, have declared me "not guilty." By it you have justified me in your sight, pardoned all my sins — past, present and future — erased my guilt and removed every penalty from my account. May I never forfeit the peace your forgiveness brings to me, and may its presence prompt me to always be forgiving of others.

DAY 24

A Heart at Peace

Let not your hearts be troubled.
John 14:27

YOUR HEART IS FICKLE. Depending on events — and
your perception of them — your heart can be hopeful
or despairing, loving or hateful, apathetic or
compassionate, conflicted or at peace, or any number
of contending emotions. And these emotions are what
complicate life.

Peace as a natural condition of the heart was forfeited
in Eden. In Scripture, the heart is the center of your
rational and emotional nature as well as the center of
your spiritual life. It is what makes you human. It is
solitary. No one can completely penetrate yours and

you cannot completely penetrate another's. Each heart knows its own bitterness, and no one else can share its joy.[1] It is the most vulnerable and fragile component of your being. It is easily broken, especially in times of disappointment and loss, and yet Jesus gently admonishes Christians: "Let not your hearts be troubled."

How can the human heart not be troubled? So why does Jesus — who knows the fickleness and challenges of the human condition — suggest something that seems unattainable?

Jesus knows your heart is the sphere of His divine influence in you. He knows it's where the Holy Spirit exercises His life-changing power, actively helping, comforting and counseling you. He knows it's the wellspring of your life.[2] He knows a heart at peace gives life to the body.[3] And He knows if you guard it above all else and entrust it to Him, it will not be troubled.

Is something troubling your heart right now? If so, guard your heart with prayer and Scripture. Lean not on your own understanding. And entrust your heart to Jesus to receive His peace.

Your heart, O God, did turn away,
So grieved by our deception.
Hearts once at peace were led astray,
To despair without exception.

Your heart, O God, did then decree,
For Jesus to restore.
Amazing grace now gives to me,
a heart at peace once more.

DAY 25

At Peace with Your Past

...and God will call the past to account.
Ecclesiastes 3:15

TIME IS AN ILLUSION. It's a human invention created to keep track of events in a linear sequence. God has no need for our concept of time, because, being both self-existent and eternal, God wasn't created. He doesn't have a beginning. God dwells in eternity but time dwells in God.[1] We, on the other hand, dwell in time – past, present and future.

Your past is prologue to your present and future. It is an intricate tapestry of positive and negative threads. In it you were formed in your mother's womb. In time, you learned all you presently know; established all the relationships you currently enjoy; acquired all the skills you now possess; experienced all the emotions you've ever felt; achieved all you've ever accomplished; survived all your failures; acquired all your biases and prejudices; obtained all your present possessions; formed your character; developed your worldview; and navigated a course that has brought you to this moment.

Are you at peace with the tapestry of your past? All of it? There are no characters in the Bible other than Jesus who did not carry negative baggage from the past sufficient to trouble their souls. Adam and Eve had The Fall. Abraham suffered from unbelief. David committed adultery and murder. Jonah feared. Peter denied Jesus. Paul murdered. Mary Magdalene was a prostitute.

The negative aspects of your past can only disturb you if they remain unredeemed. To be at peace with the parts of your past that trouble your soul, you must be forgiven and redeemed by Jesus Christ. Once forgiven and redeemed, the negative baggage from your past can be used by God for your benefit and His glory.

Father God, thank you for my past. It represents our history together. You have been with me all along, even in the days when I didn't know you, even when you seemed far away. But your unseen hand was always guiding, providing and protecting. Your goodness has given me joys and your redemption brings peace to my past.

DAY 26

At Peace with Your Future

A man cannot discover anything about his future.
Ecclesiastes 7:14

Therefore, do not worry about tomorrow…
Matthew 6:34

"NEVER BE AFRAID TO TRUST AN UNKNOWN FUTURE to a known God." This encouragement comes from Corrie ten Boom who spent ten months in a Nazi concentration camp during World War II for hiding over 800 Jews hunted by the Nazi Gestapo. Trusting God was indispensible to ten Boom's being at peace with her future.

As a Christian, you have a future that is both temporal and eternal. God has set eternity in your heart,[1] but because of The Fall, you are forced to dwell in time. So to be at peace with your temporal future, you must trust God's character. To be at peace with your eternal future, you must trust God's promises and prophecies.

We are uncomfortable with the unknown, so we're always anticipating what's to come, straining to see beyond the horizon of the present. But our mind's eye either collapses from exhaustion or surrenders to frustration or fear. Would you be doing this if you fully entrusted all your tomorrows to God's character? Scripture says God is faithful, just and trustworthy.[2] To be at peace with your temporal future, you must look to God's character, knowing He will never leave you or forsake you.[3]

Beyond your temporal future lies your eternal future. God's prophecies tell us that since The Fall, human history has been moving toward a divinely ordained goal: a new earth inhabited by people redeemed through Jesus Christ who will live eternally in a world with no more crying, no more death, no more mourning, and no more pain;[4] giving God praise in glorified, resurrected bodies. Put your trust in God's prophecies to be at peace with your eternal future.

It is in your character and promises, Father God, that I put my trust for the future. You are never-changing, loving, all-powerful, and all-knowing. Your promises have been thoroughly tested and you are faithful to each one. I must trust in the character of your promises and in the promises of your character to be at peace with my future.

Day 27

At Peace with Your Present

I have learned to be content whatever the circumstances.
Philippians 4:11

W HETHER IT IS THE BEST OF TIMES or the worst of times, the present is the only time you have.[1] And while your present is inextricably intertwined with your past, it's not necessarily bound by it. While sitting in a Roman prison, the Apostle Paul wrote to the Christians in Philippi that he learned to be content whatever his circumstances — both past and present. Paul's circumstances included beatings, riots, sleepless nights, distress and hunger.

Worldly contentment is marked by feelings of satisfaction, assuredness and safety. It's an "in the moment," transient condition where you don't remember past anxieties, project future ones or wrestle with contending thoughts. One of my seminary professors referred to this type of contentment as "achieving cognitive rest." Nevertheless, this shouldn't be confused with divine contentment and God's peace.

Divine contentment, the kind experienced by Paul as he sat in prison, is the result of God's hand on your life, and is what makes it possible for you to be at peace with your present. The Greek word Paul uses to signify contentment means raising up a barrier to ward off a threat. Whatever the circumstances, he tells the Philippians, his peace is undisturbed because a barrier has been raised up to protect it. That barrier is Jesus Christ — the Lord of peace — the one who gives peace at all times and in every way.[2]

God's peace and contentment are abiding. They are not circumstantial. Like His mercies, they are new every morning. They are refreshing to the soul and give you the opportunity to acknowledge the blessings you have received and honor the One who gave them.

Being at peace with your present comes from your position of being in Christ, not "in the moment" contentment.

Father God, this present moment is the time:

> *To praise you;*
> *To consider your glory and majesty;*
> *To count myself dead to sin but alive to you in*
> * Christ Jesus;*
> *To give thanks in all my circumstances, for this is your*
> * will for me in Christ Jesus;*
> *To contemplate your call to love you and others with all*
> * my heart, soul, mind and strength;*
> *To be content with only those things that come from you.*

Make my soul thirst for you in this moment, so I may be at peace with my present.

DAY 28

Peace in the Midst of Change

…you are a new creation…
2 Corinthians 5:17

Our daughter, Bryn, was only 4 years old when she declared: "This is not how I expected my life to turn out!" Something in her young life had changed and she wasn't at peace with it.

Adults understand this even more acutely. We are comfortable with the familiar. The familiar is where we know what to do, know how to feel, know what to expect, know how to act, know how to respond, know what to control, know what to manipulate, and know how to survive. Such beacons of certainty and comfort are rarely present when we encounter change so disorienting it dislocates our bearing with the familiar and threatens to disturb our peace were Jesus not in the midst of it.

And yet the constant in our lives is change.

Each season of our lives is different. People change emotionally, physically, spiritually and mentally. There is change we initiate and change over which we have no control. Some change is good, some is bad. And some change is so forceful it touches the core of our being — our identity, our thinking, and our outlook on life. Sanctification is that kind of change.

Sanctification, the most dramatic change you will experience this side of eternity, is the process of Jesus transforming you into His likeness.[1] And as the Holy Spirit changes your inner life, he'll enable you to undertake good works that are different in moral quality from those performed by people who haven't been regenerated by God's Spirit.

Sanctification is mortifying. It requires the crucifixion of who you were.[2] But you can rest in the fact that the Holy Spirit is orchestrating the process in a way that brings peace in the midst of the change.

Thank you for the change.
Thank you for the difference.
Thank you for your love.
Thank you for the stillness.
Thank you for a heart that's knowing
Your Spirit is sowing, peace in the midst of change.

DAY 29

Rest in Peace

"My Presence will go with you, and I will give you rest."
Exodus 33:14

"Come to me, all you who are weary and burdened,
and I will give you rest."
Matthew 11:28

HERE'S A LIE: People who are completely booked and always in demand at work, home and church are worthy of admiration.

Here's the truth: Often those pursuits are out of balance, and these people are restless victims of the busy trap.

Jonathan Edwards, one of America's most-gifted Christian theologians, observed a vast difference between the peace Christians experience and the "peace of the world." The peace of the world, he said, is founded in blindness and delusion, but a Christian's peace comes from having open eyes to see things as they truly are.[1] According to Edwards, Christians find peace and rest in the reality of their salvation, future resurrection and eternal life, while those without Christ must remain ignorant of what is true concerning God and themselves in order to remain satisfied with the fleeting peace found in worldly pursuits.

The things of this world cannot give true peace and rest to the soul. Even the best of them are but empty shadows, and pursuing them deprives the soul of the much-needed rest God prescribes for a well-balanced life. After God created the universe and everything in it, He rested to enjoy what He had accomplished.[2] He exhorts you to do the same.[3]

You need rest from life's demands and pressures and not just rest of mind and body. You need inner rest of the soul. God's most peaceful rest comes to your soul when you cease work for one day each week to enjoy God, to reflect on what He has enabled you to accomplish, and to cherish the freedom you have in Christ. Busyness is a form of slavery, and "Sabbath Rest"[4] is the emancipator. Jesus is Lord of the Sabbath[5] — the Lord of rest! In Him you can rest in peace.

In your shadow, Almighty God, is the glorious dwelling place of rest, a shelter from life's demands and pressures. You let the weary rest in it. Your people live in a fortress of rest, where hearts are glad and tongues rejoice. Your Spirit directs us to the right path and prompts us to walk in it because the promise of entering your rest still stands. Anyone who enters your rest also rests from his own work, just as you did from yours. Carry me — poised and restful — in the flow of your living water so I may today rest in peace.

DAY 30

Making Peace

Blessed are the peacemakers…
Matthew 5:9

Peacemakers who sow in peace raise
a harvest of righteousness.
James 3:18

ON MARCH 31, 1978, I HAD THE HONOR of spending a few moments with the former U.S. Secretary of State Henry Kissinger. Talking with a world leader who'd received the Nobel Peace Prize for his role in ending the Vietnam War by negotiating the Paris Peace Accords was quite a memorable encounter.

Sixteen hundred years earlier, Roman Emperor Constantine the Great convened the Council of Nicaea in 325 A.D., to address a controversy over Jesus' divinity. To the assembled delegates representing all of Christendom, Constantine said: "Discord in the church I consider more fearful and painful than any other war...Delay not therefore...servants of God; put away all causes of strife, and loose all knots of discord by the laws of peace."[1]

Although Kissinger and Constantine were peacemakers at very different moments in history, they shared a common understanding: Making peace is more important than keeping peace.

Keeping peace doesn't alter the dynamics of a controversy; it just tinkers with the nuts and bolts. Peacekeeping is simply monitoring or policing terms imposed by another, and it may not even require cooperation, collaboration or interaction among the disputants.

Making peace involves changing the very structure of the relationship or the environment, touching on values, beliefs and behaviors. It's an internal change that requires us to alter deeply held beliefs, modify established habits and behaviors and transform the way we think.

As you fulfill your calling to love God and others, and as you serve where your love for God intersects with the needs of people, be an agent of Jesus' peace; making peace as you go so all that you sow raises a harvest of righteousness.

Lord Jesus, you bless those who are peacemakers in this world and call them your children. May you, the Lord of peace, give them peace at all times and in every way. May I be an agent of your peace, serving where my love for you intersects with the needs of people and making peace as I go in order to sow a harvest of righteousness.

DAY 31

Go in Peace

Jesus said to the woman,
"Your faith has saved you; go in peace."
Luke 7:50

Then he said to her,
"Daughter, your faith has healed you. Go in peace."
Luke 8:48

THE PROSTITUTE APPROACHES JESUS in the middle of a dinner party. Falling at His feet, she wets them with her tears. She then wipes them with her hair, kisses them and pours perfume on them.[1] On another occasion, a woman suffering from a hemorrhage for 12 years reaches out and touches Jesus' clothes as He walks through a crowded street.[2] For both women it is their faith in Jesus that prompts them to come to Him.

For the first woman, it's faith that only Jesus can save her. For the second woman, it's faith that only Jesus can heal her. Jesus acknowledges their faith by saving the first and healing the second. And to both of them He says: "Go in peace."

What an intriguing command! Why doesn't Jesus tell the first woman, "Go in your salvation," or the second, "Go in your healing"? After all, these are the things the women came for and received. Why, "Go in peace"?

For both of these women, neither prostitution nor illness is the issue. Their issue is anxious and weary hearts, lives lived apart from Jesus. Jesus says, "Come to me, all you who are weary and burdened, and I will give you rest." Peace is a by-product of coming to Jesus, of living life in Him, regardless of the circumstances. And just as He said to the women, Jesus will say to you — once you lay all at His feet —

"Go in peace." And not just for peace in the moment, but for a continuous peace as you travel through life's journey, resting secure in the knowledge that God will never leave you or forsake you.[3]

Your Spirit alone, Lord Jesus, instructs me and teaches me in the way I should go. Help me to go in peace, whether I'm being led beside quiet waters, guided in paths of righteousness, or walking through the valley of the shadow of death, knowing you will never leave me or forsake me.

NOTES

Day 1

    1. 2 Chronicles 14:2-6

Day 2

    1. Proverbs 14:30

Day 3

    1. Colossians 1:16

Day 4

    1. Psalm 13:2
    2. Romans 8:6
    3. Philippians 4:8

Day5

    1. 2 Samuel 11:1-26
    2. John 16:33
    3. Colossians 3:15

Day 6

    1. John 21:15-18
    2. I Corinthians 14:1
    3. I Corinthians 13
    4. Galatians 5:6

Day 7

    1. The ESV® Bible (The Holy Bible, English Standard Version®) copyright © 2001 by Crossway, a publishing ministry of Good News Publishers. ESV® Text Edition: 2011.
    2. 1 Corinthians 13
    3. Philippians 4:7
    4. Revelation 21:1-4

Day 8

    1. Billy Graham, *A Biblical Standard For Evangelists* (Charlotte: Worldwide Publications, 1984) 20.

Day 9

    1. John 14:16-20

    2. Ecclesiastes 8:14

    3. Proverbs 16:9

Day 11

    1. Matt 20:28

    2. Mark 10:43-44

    3. Oswald Chambers, *My Utmost for His Highest* (New York: Dodd, Mead & Company, 1935) 10.

    4. 1 Peter 4:10

Day 12

    1. Mark 12:30-31

    2. Chris Payne, sermon at New Charlotte Church, 2012.

    3. John T. McNeill, ed. *Institutes of the Christian Religion 1*, by John Calvin, trans. Ford Lewis Battles (Louisville: Westminster John Knox Press, 1960) paraphrase 840.

Day 13

    1. Proverbs 19:21

    2. Isaiah 46:10

Day 14

1. Acts 17:28

Day 15

    1. Augustine of Hippo, *Confessions*, trans. Henry Chadwick (New York: Oxford University Press, 1998) 105.

    2. Genesis 3:22

    3. Ecclesiastes 7:1

    4. 1 Corinthians 15:55

Day 16
1. Hebrews 10:24-25
2. Ephesians 4:3

Day 17
1. Proverbs 17:22

Day 18
1. Matthew 5-7
2. John 3:5-8
3. Matthew 6:33

Day 19
1. A.W. Tozer, *The Knowledge of the Holy* (New York: Waller and Company, 1996), 1.

Day 20
1. "Quotations about Time," last modified January 24, 2014, http://www.quotegarden.com/time.html.

Day 22
1. Galatians 5:22
2. Galatians 5:19-21

Day 23
1. "I'm Still Learning to Forgive" by Corrie ten Boom. *Guideposts Magazine.* 1972.
2. Matthew 6:15
3. Colossians 3:13
4. Colossians 3:15

Day 24
1. Proverbs 14:10
2. Proverbs 4:23
3. Proverbs 14:30

Day 25
1. A.W. Tozer, *The Knowledge of the Holy*, Waller and Company, New York. 1961. 72.

Day 26

1. Ecclesiastes 3:11
2. Psalm 111:7
3. Hebrews 13:5
4. Revelation 21:4

Day 27

1. Paraphrase of "Whether it's the best of times or the worst of times, it's the only time we've got." Art Buchwald, American humorist, http://www.brainyquote.com/quotes/quotes/a/artbuchwal104437.html#YvOm88uIIBdzllTo.99.

2. 2 Thessalonians 3:16

Day 28

1. 2 Corinthians 3:18
2. Romans 6:6

Day 29

1. Jonathan Edwards, "The Peace Which Christ Gives His True Followers," *Selected Writings of Jonathan Edwards*, ed. Harold P. Simonson (Long Grove: Waveland Press, Inc., 2004) 99-104.

2. Genesis 1:31
3. Deuteronomy 5:13-14
4. Hebrews 4:9
5. Mark 2:27-28

Day 30

1. *Christian Classics Ethereal Library, History of the Christian Church, Volume III: Nicene and Post-Nicene Christianity. A.D. 311-600.* http://www.ccel.org/ccel/schaff/hcc3.iii.xii.iv.html. Accessed 2/16/14.

Day 31

1. Luke 7:36-50
2. Luke 8:43-48
3. Hebrews 13:5

About the Author

Neil Carmichael is an executive with one of the world's largest dispute resolution organizations. Throughout his professional career, he has been involved in providing arbitration and mediation services to individuals, corporations, churches and ministries. Neil holds a Master of Arts degree from Reformed Theological Seminary and lives in Charlotte, N.C., where he is a volunteer staff member for PeacePoint Ministry. He and his wife, Barbara, are the proud parents of two adult children, Aaron and Bryn. Neil can be reached at neil@peacepoint.com.